C mom work®

{*See* yourself living the life you've always dreamed of by using the skills and talents being a mom has blessed you with. Making life *work* to the best of your ability.}

A C mom is

Creating the best possible world in which they raise their children while nurturing the best possible scenarios for themselves and families by using the skills and talent motherhood has blessed them with.

A C mom

Constantly adapts and designs their ideal life situation while *working* on manifesting their dreams.

A C mom is

Sharing their successes and inspirations with other moms who need help in realizing their own dreams.

A C mom

Wants her children to *see mom work* towards her goals, dreams and true-life purpose so they can learn by example.

Are you a C mom?

Join our C mom work community now!
LIKE US ON FACE BOOK @ C MOM WORK
Follow us on Twitter

C mom work, its contents and illustrations are registered under U.S. trademark serial number 77755660 06/09/2009. All rights reserved. No part of this publication may be reproduced, store in or introduced into a retrieval system, or transmitted, in any form or by any means (electronic, mechanical, photocopying, recording or otherwise), without the prior written permission of the trademark owner. The scanning uploading, and distribution of this book via the Internet or via any other means without permission of the trademark owner is illegal and punishable by law.

www.cmomwork.com

Table of Contents

- C mom work Introduction — p.5
- A is for ASPIRE — p.6
- B is for BELIEVE — p.9
- C is for CREATE — p.11
- D is for DREAM — p.13
- E is for EMBRACE — p.16
- F is for FORGIVENESS — p.18
- G is for GRATITUDE — p.20
- H is for HARMONIZE — p.22
- I is for INTUIT — p.24
- J is for JOY — p.26
- K is for KINDNESS — p.28
- L is for LOVELINESS — p.30
- M is for MEDITATION — p.32
- N is for NOURISH — p.34
- O is for OPEN — p.36
- P is for PRANA — p.38
- Q is for QUIETUDE — p.41
- R is for REVIVE — p.43
- S is for SPIRITUALITY — p.45
- T is for TRANSFORM — p.47
- U is for UNITY — p.50
- V is for VIGILANCE — p.52
- W is for WISDOM — p.55
- X is for eXPLORE — p.57
- Y is for YOUTHFULNESS — p.60
- Z is for ZERO — p.62

Author

Valarie Anderson runs a media company and was the first female publisher of the Los Angeles Times Sunday Magazine and also their Fashion Director. Her career spans over 20 years in Fashion Luxury publishing. She has her B.A. in English and has published poetry and magazine articles. She resides in Palos Verdes California with her son and husband.

Illustrator

Sheri Kuller has two kids, one is her husband and the other is her son. The Computer frustrates her. Her teeny, tiny house is always messy and bugs freak her out. She is fascinated with nineteenth century England, a huge fan of Junior Golf, potato chips and misty days. She loves her family completely, her friends more than they know and of course, loves to draw.

Introduction

{*See* yourself living the life you've always dreamed of by using the skills and talents being a mom has blessed you with. Making life *work* to the best of your ability.}

Moms' aspirations and dreams didn't fly out the window the day the stork arrived. They just got pushed aside with the day-to-day of motherhood demands. As creators, moms are prewired to design whatever life they want for themselves and their families. It's time again, to focus on the bigger picture of the status of mom and the powerful influence moms have on our children's lives, their communities and society in general. C mom work is designed to remind moms of their dreams and goals and to help moms take the first steps toward living the life they always dreamed of having.

C mom work aspires moms to create the best possible world in which to raise their children while nurturing the best scenarios for themselves and families. C moms can be the sole income providers, equal income providers or zero income providers in their household. C moms constantly adapt and design their ideal working situation. Let's not limit the word "work" to the status of "job". In this book the word work means to function fully, to live true and operate well and at the maximum levels, for yourself and kids. Happy moms are successful moms and successful moms raise successful children-that then build successful communities.

Moms, all over the world, at some time in their "mom" career, struggle with how to "work" better. I know I have. I've worked full time and part time. I've been an independent contractor and a stay at home mom. I've worked in the glamorous and competitive world of international fashion magazine publishing and have scrubbed toilets at midnight to supplement my income. I've been over paid, under paid and not paid at all. I've been married, divorced, single and married again and the most important thing I've learned along the way is how to manifest the world I want and need, for myself and child, at any given time in the mom-cycle. I've learned to work it to the best of my ability while upgrading those abilities along the way.

I am not an expert, feminist, child psychologist, workaholic or a celebrity. The motivation for C mom work is, like all moms I want the best for my child and the world while maximizing my full potentiality. I've learned a few tricks that have inspired me and I've been inspired by others to reach those goals.

The desire to share my experience and help a mom or two while presenting an A to Z of aspirations beautifully illustrated by my co-C mom conspirator Sheri Kuller is part of creating the world we want right now at this point in our C mom lives.

A

ASPIRE: {To long, aim or seek ambitiously, especially for something great or of a higher value.}

Aspire to have all areas of your life working better, feeling fantastic, harboring happiness and languishing in the love you were meant to give and receive. Aspirations are crucial fodder for dream weaving and idealism.

Aspiring towards personal greatness and all the wonderful things that means as individuals and moms can be as simplistic as trying to act nicer or as complex as striving to be the first in your field. Soar towards the stars and reach for greater heights of aspiration that fuel your soul and immortalize your ideals. Miraculous moments are to be had here and now.

By concentrating on everyday aspirations meaningful to you, your chances for living true to yourself and in harmony with your desires and obligations are more abundant. Aspirations jump start your manifest destiny and probe you towards acting out your desires and dreams. Become an aspirant of elevating your life purpose, your role as a mother and the tremendous effect that can have on the whole of humanity. There are no limits to what you can aspire to except what your own doubts can conger up. Thankfully, desires are much stronger than doubts if they come from the heart, so cast your line and expect to reel in the biggest catch your heart desires.

Our lives take on more meaning and richness from the struggle towards betterment and benefit from fantasies of higher purpose and ideals.

As moms, our altruism finds roots in love and hope and creation. See the vast potential children have in front of them and let it be an aspirational motivator for the rest of your life too. Use your children as your aspirational angels. Let them remind you of who you really are when you are at your best and of the power that love has to transform.

If we have nothing noble to aspire to, what are we doing here and how does our life take on meaning?

That's what I was asking myself as I drove out of the executive parking structure I had occupied for the last time. The past 18 months were nothing to aspire to. Sure, there was the big title (well, actually 2) and the accompanying salary, which was nothing to sneeze at and the most I had ever made. However, the tired and newly lined face, the stressed out physical body that was completely drained, the lack of sleep, blackberry addiction and numerous red-eyes across the country were surely nothing to aspire to. The time away from the people I cherish: my son and husband, the friends who were patient with once or twice a year interactions because I was never home or available, the incessant projects that needed always to be better and more profitable, the countless hours in traffic, the horrendous people I had to suck up to-Enough already! I was glad to be out and able to examine what I really wanted again.

As a recent former publisher of products that were meant to be aspirational for one million people on Sunday morning, I knew it was now my new job to find out what aspirations I had for me. It was only natural that my quick reflection led me to the thing that I am most proud of being: a mom. Sounds corny, but of all the accomplishments in my life, the one true aspiration that has motivated me to reach my highest potential was because of the child who was watching me along the way. I wanted to be the very best person I could be at the time, for him. That doesn't mean perfect by any measure and the mistakes were, and are still, a big part of the journey.

My aspirations are based in our mother-child relationship and all the amazing possibilities that can entail for both of us.

Being aware of those tiny growing people who watch us up close and from afar, with wonder and dependency, puts us on personal guard to be ever vigilant of our motivations, hopes and dreams, since they are usually, in some way, included in them. Realize how fundamentally organic a role your children play in inspiring you towards being a bigger, better, more loving and happy version of yourself and unlock all that amazing potential to live the best life you can.

B

BELIEVE: {To have confidence in the truth, existence, reliability or value of something.}

Believe that you can have whatever world you want for you and your child. Really believe it, in your gut, your desires, your dreams, and in every action you take.
If you don't believe that you are the author of your own life story, then the rest of this encyclopedia is useless. Nothing will work if you don't believe it can in the first place. This sounds pretty basic, but you'd be surprised at how often we are programmed not to believe.

I'm not talking about positive thinking, which is great, but useless if there is not an ingrained belief system that you really can create your own life. I am talking about the ability within yourself to know that you can achieve whatever you want.

I wasn't born with this ability. Like most people, I had to learn it and trial and error was my teacher. The more I played with manifesting and bringing into reality what I wanted, the more I learned that just believing that I was going to get it was half the battle. Really believing.

Experiment and start with believing in something small. Believe that you will get flowers this week. Really believe it. Expect it. Plan for those flowers to come. Make sure you have a clean vase for their arrival, pick out a spot to put them. Picture them in that spot. Really believe you are getting those flowers. Don't get specific with the details. Just believe in the power of your thoughts. See what happens. It shouldn't take more than a week to have those flowers appear. There's no room for doubt here so practice until you see those flowers manifest.

Do you believe you deserve what you want? Do you believe you are capable of creating it? Do you believe that if you put your mind to something and focus on it you can achieve it? These are questions you have to deeply examine and it may be surprising to find out the answers. Action follows thought, so no inherent belief system equals no outcome.

I think for many years I didn't believe I deserved to live a certain way without depending on someone else providing it for me. Although I have held a job since I was 14 years old, I don't think I ever really believed I could create what I wanted because I didn't believe I deserved it. I didn't think I was worthy of it. No matter how much money I made, or things I accomplished, I believed I needed validation elsewhere. The day I discovered I was pregnant, all that disbelief transformed. A shift towards the truly creative side of life emerged and I believed that I could do anything!

If you don't believe in yourself you can't create the life you want for yourself. It's that easy. So start believing in "You". It's the fuel that runs the creative process and the foundation for manifesting your desires. Your children believe in you and put great trust in the belief that you are an all-powerful force (until they hit their teens). So garner that belief in your own abilities and see what transpires from the empowering effects of believing you can.

C

CREATE: {To cause to come into being, as something unique.}

Create your world, create your life, create your story and be the author of your own epic novel. When you create your own life and live it to the fullest, it follows that your children will see and learn how to do the same thing. If you simply go along with what comes your way, you are teaching your kids to do the same thing by example. Our children are smart and see so much.

C moms are constantly creating. Yes, life is going to give you challenges and heartaches, obstacles and pitfalls, but what you create out of those situations is what matters. Sometimes those challenges result in the best growth opportunity or valuable life lessons you can learn. Create something you want out of life's lessons. That's what they are there for.

I was going through a divorce when my son was five years old. I decided to start a new life for the two of us. I never thought I would be a divorced single mom. I had an executive job in fashion advertising and had security in a good paycheck and benefits. I am not the type that believes in hosing your ex, so I was fully committed to supporting my son and me. The only problem was that I wanted to be there full-time for my child. My job and hour-long commute just didn't allow for that. Yikes, at that time, my big corporate job didn't even want me mentioning I had a child at all. However, I knew somehow I could create a job with the status and income I deserved, while being there for my child after school as well, and I created it out of this inherent belief that I could have it.

Eventually, I was headhunted by a European magazine that needed a U.S. publisher to represent them in the states while they globalized the magazine. Even though the status of the magazine was well below the reputation of the "corporate giant" I was currently employed by, I took the interview. I immediately saw the opportunity to create a really important magazine in the industry while creating the lifestyle I needed at home. Since I would be working for Europeans on an eight-hour time difference and the majority of the work was done during early morning hours. The nine to five pit fall that every working mom faces was eliminated.

I worked before my child woke up and after he slept. I worked while he was in school during business hours. I worked harder and more creatively because I worked waiting in the car during soccer practice and on the weekends when he was with his dad. I ran the North American branch of a large European publisher and I did it without the assistance of a nanny.

Of course there was give and take to the job and I took on more responsibility and personal liability than a regular corporate job entails, but the business acumen and skills I learned by just being given the opportunity to do them has propelled me into a whole new category of business expertise that I would never have experienced otherwise.

I also created new projects and products for the company that helped their production as a result of being such a happily working C mom.

Create your life, your lifestyle and your dreams. The more energy you put into creating what you desire, the more opportunity comes your way to live in an even bigger and better way. Initially, I didn't know the details of creating this better life, but I believed it existed. I spent a lot of mental time creating the idea that my child and I could have it.

D

DREAM: {An ideal, an aspiration, goal or aim. To see or imagine.}

Dream big! Don't hold back. This is your life and the only one you have right now so give it all you've got. Look to your children for the right inspiration when you dream. Watch how they play and enliven their games with their unyielding ability to dream and imagine whatever they want. Take their cue and begin to dream up your fantasy mom life.

Spend a few days or weeks formulating your dream. Learn about your true desires and juxtapose them with the obligations that motherhood entails.

Before you go to sleep every night, ask the angels, God, or whomever you place your faith in to help you formulate your dreams. Visualize your dreams, refining and reshaping them as you progress. Picture yourself working out your dream in as much detail as possible and keep a notebook by your bed in case you wake with any new information or points of view regarding your dreams. Write the information down so you can remember it later. When you wake up in the morning, spend a few minutes in bed reliving your dream. You will be amazed at how wonderfully this process works to give you a restful and healthy sleep too.

When you think you have the shape of your dream intact, take a full day-spent alone- to make your dream wheel. Your dream wheel helps clarify your dream intentions and keeps your dreams at the forefront of your mind, so you can accomplish them.

Make sure you are in a happy mood when you go to create your dream wheel. Play your favorite music, light a candle, set the mood of bliss to make your wheel. This is extremely important because your mood weaves itself into the actual wheel as you make it. Just like cooking, the more love your pour into this project the better it will turn out.

To make your wheel you need some pretty red paper the shape and size of a medium, round pizza. Red is a great color to help manifest your dreams. Sit facing north. You don't want things going "south" or bad. Make sure your creating space is clear of clutter, and chaos. Partition your red wheel into 12 sections-12 separate parts of equal size with a pencil or marker. Get creative and make it attractive to you. Starting at 9 O'clock label each section working clockwise with the following categories:

9 o'clock	Your appearance, sense of self
10 o'clock	Your finances and tangible assets
11 o'clock	Written and oral communications
12 o'clock	Your home
1 o'clock	Creativity, your children, romance
2 o'clock	Your health and charity
3 o'clock	Your partnerships and or marriage
4 o'clock	Your sexuality and patience and tolerance
5 o'clock	Higher education, publishing and foreign trips
6 o'clock	Your reputation and or fame
7 o'clock	Your friends and associates
8 o'clock	Your subconscious and psychic abilities

After you have your dream wheel labeled, fill each section with a magazine picture or drawing, or scrapbook image or even words that represent your dream for that section. Pick imagery that resonates with you, even if you don't exactly know why you are picking it. It's amazing how the universe sometimes knows how to give us the things we want. For example, if you want a new home, put a picture of a home that best matches what you want in the 12 o'clock section. Take your time and have fun with your dream wheel. Try not to clutter it up too much.

After you're done (it takes longer than you think), hang your dream wheel on a north-facing wall. Your dream wheel is your creation and should be kept away from public eyes. It is good to stand facing north when you look at it, which is what you are going to do every day. This helps you to visualize your dreams and keeps you focused and on target with what you want. Spend a few minutes looking at all the lovely images of your dreamscape every day. Be happy when you look at your wheel and try to project loving energy towards your dream objectives.

When an area of your dream wheel is accomplished, you must give back to the universe in that area. Let's go back to the new home dream. You get the home. The first thing you should do is give some money, volunteer or find a way to help someone who is in need of a new home. This is very important because it keeps the dream energy flowing. What you take in you must give back. It's natural law. If you only inhale and never exhale you impale the natural law of cycle. Work your dreams back into your life so you can fully experience the natural cycle you were born to contribute to.

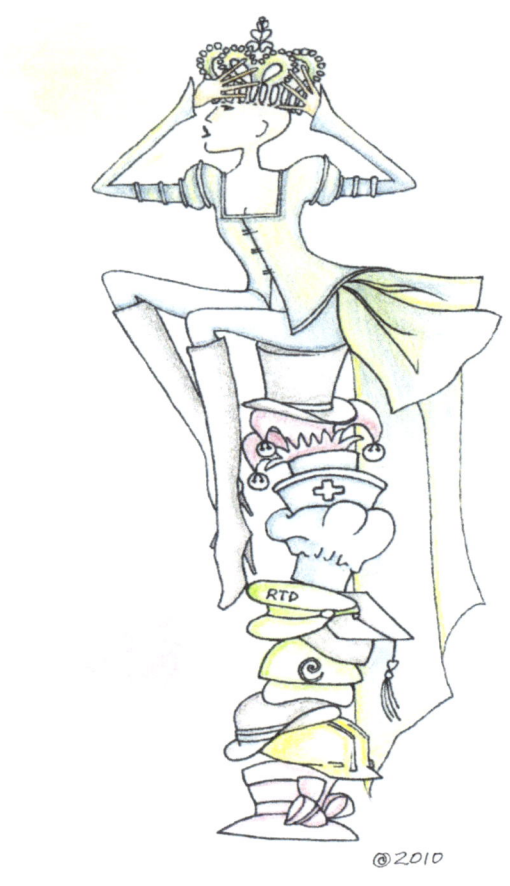

E

EMBRACE: {To take or receive gladly or eagerly, accept willing.}

Embrace life as a mom with all its good qualities and all its not-so-good qualities. Wrap your arms around the total picture of what being a mom is all about for you. By embracing the whole big picture of your life accurately and seeing it for all it's flaws and perks, you'll be better equipped to steer your life in the direction you need it to go.

Embrace the natural cycles of life and learn from the ebb and flow of the highs and lows that life inevitably throws your way. By embracing the natural energy flow of the life cycle, you tend to be more prepared for the low points. By being more prepared mentally and even physically for the low points, you'll find its easier to get through them. Don't get stuck in the quagmire of thinking a particular time in your life is permanent. Nothing is permanent and eventually the tide has got to change in your favor. That's the law of cycle.

The same works on the positive side of things. Don't just assume that your happy-go- lucky life will remain that way permanently. Assume nothing. Prepare for the lows when you are at the top of the positive curve of the cycle. Embrace your whole sense of being by taking inventory from time to time on where you are in the cycle. Appreciate the good points and notice how amazingly rewarding the small little details are.

For example, if you happen to be in a good place in your life, let everyone know and feel that from you. Let the "goodness" flow into everything you do and into everyone you encounter. By doing this, you are preparing to make it through the low points. Because of the natural cycle of things, the goodness will return to you when you most need it. It has to. The good energy is following the natural laws of cycle.

We tend to hold onto the precious moments of our lives with a ferocity that stifles them. By embracing those moments gently and tenderly we give them enough room for inclusion and growth and expansion.

F

FORGIVENESS: {To cease to feel resentment against. To pardon an offense or a mistake.}

Forgiveness is at the real heart of success. If moms didn't forgive, they couldn't make it past the childbirth state!

Mothers are wonderful forgivers and could teach the world leaders a thing or two about the effectiveness of forgiving one another. The inherent principal of teaching your baby, child, teenager or young adult is the capacity to forgive mistakes.

Mothers are excellent at forgiving their children, but how big of a part does forgiveness play in other areas of your life?

As good as women are at forgiving, they are just as good at resentment and even better at holding grudges. Resentment and holding on to life's small indignations is absolutely useless in the C mom vocabulary. It simply has no useful place any time, because it has no positive affect or outcome- ever.

For the sake of efficiency, forgiveness is the easier task at hand. We don't grudge our children into learning; we forgive them into it.

Forgiveness should never be confused with being a doormat. It should be viewed as a virtue. Look at forgiveness as grace in action. Everyone makes mistakes and no one is exempt. Forgiving people for making mistakes is actually a very selfish process if you break it down. X does harm to you, you don't forgive X and you harbor ill feelings towards X. Those ill feelings stay within you to attract more negativity. You are eventually harmed by them- whether they show up physically, or as an outburst or just a small thorn that surfaces when you least expect it. The longer you don't forgive a person, the stickier the ill feelings become. By forgiving someone, you are free and clear to capture the more empowering qualities you want to attract. You are doing yourself a favor by shaking off the event.

Doormats are created by not learning the lessons of the negative event that required your forgiveness in the first place. Doormats re-experience the same events repeatedly. You can forgive but it doesn't mean you let the same thing happen to you again. This is crucial and is what separates the doormats from the forgivers.

So forgive and forget, but learn the lesson. Forgive yourself of your past mistakes. Remember that you are constantly evolving and learning. Don't be afraid to teach your children that you are learning too. It lets them see mom in a different light and gives permission for failures. With the pressures of today's society and push for perfection, forgiveness is the release valve that says its OK to screw up as long as you learn something within the process. This is invaluable for children and teaches them tolerance along the way.

Practice forgiveness every day before you go to sleep and ask that you be forgiven for any offenses you may have caused that day as well. The myth of the perfect mom is just that. Everyone makes mistakes.

For years I was resentful of an unsuccessful marriage. I was lucky enough to have someone point out to me the damage that this was quietly creating in my life. The moment I started really trying to forgive myself, my ex-husband, and the situation, things changed dramatically. Communications became easier and high-intensity situations became almost nonexistent. It's an internal process and doesn't need to be reciprocated or even discussed with the parties involved. We aren't talking reality show catharsis but a quiet contemplation of releasing harmful indignation, small slights and hurt feelings. Forgiveness is truly grace in action.

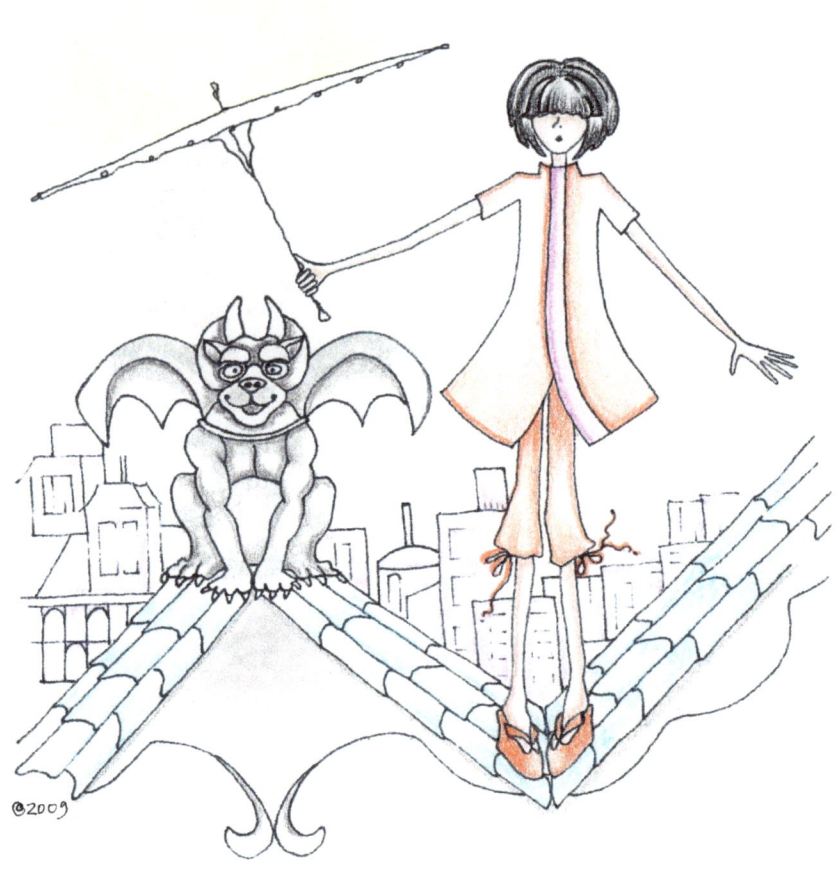

G

GRATITUDE: {The quality of feeling warmly or deeply appreciative or thankful}.

Gratitude. Not attitude. Sometimes we are so lost in our own soup of insecurities that we surround ourselves with a wall of self-protection.
We think this wall protects us from looking vulnerable, weak or out of control but it actually absorbs those qualities into our state of being and attracts similar energy.

It's a vicious cycle that is impervious to constructive criticism, inner reflection and sometimes even much-needed help. It's also a cycle that can be broken with gratitude.

Gratitude is the essence of a C mom. With children we have so much to be grateful for. Are they healthy, well fed, happy? The simplicity of being grateful in your heart for the simplest of pleasures shows the universe that you are ready for greater pleasures. Gratitude when things go wrong mitigates the expansiveness of injustice. Being grateful for life, breath, air and sunshine, when all else around you seems dark, helps you to pull in more of the lightness in life, narrowing the void of the not-so-good.

Expressing gratitude is one of the most positive things you can do daily for people around you, including loved ones and even strangers, and most of the time it doesn't cost a dime. A smile given to the check-out cashier, a nod of appreciation to the overworked teacher, an unexpected and uninitiated hug for your husband are so easy to give and can show how truly grateful you are for those around you. Gratitude puts meaning into your life in the most effortless way. Use it often and in large quantities with sincerity and intensity.

A gracious heart is a happy heart, and in a world where children are raised with instant gratification, the role model you are constructing while showing gratitude often is one that creates satisfied and greed-free children. The level of one-upmanship has turned our society into a revolving door of gimme-getme's because not enough people are grateful. No sooner do we fulfill our desire than we move on to the next one. We wonder why it's never enough-the house needs to be bigger, the car newer, the face and body younger, but it isn't making us more satisfied, peaceful or happy because somewhere along the way we forgot to be grateful and live and show our gratitude.

Be grateful for another day and chance to express yourself in the world and to your children. If necessary, list the things you are grateful for, go feed the hungry if you're really blue. The numerous things you should be grateful for will appear before your eyes immediately. You will magically remember the gifts you've been given. Visit an elder relative and see how your company alone is a gracious gift to another. Be grateful for the time you have left to make a difference in the world. Be a beacon of gratitude in a world of have and have-nots and see how the goodness comes back to you en masse.

H

HARMONIZE: {To bring into form a complete and consistent whole, to be congruous.}

Harmonize your work with your pleasure. Mix your tasks with your enjoyments. Accentuate the ordinary with the extraordinary. Play with the monotonous. Enchant the mundane. Tempt the tedious with imagination and ingenuity.

Harmonizing your life is like balancing your checkbook. It's a necessity that gives you information on where you're at, what's coming in and what's going out or what's already gone. Once you start mastering it, you start to have fun with it.

This is where your efficiency level increases with your enjoyment level. Before you know it, you can't tell the difference between the work and the play. Harmonizing is good, old-fashioned making the most of what you have. Especially when what you have, as a C mom, is a lack of time.

Here are some good examples of harmonizing your life:

*Crank up your iPod and dance while you do the laundry. (Also gives you a mini workout).

*Listen to audio books, self-help books or learn a new language while driving to the office or waiting in line for school pick up.

*Pay your bills while getting a pedicure.

*Penalize bad attitudes and behavior by making your children clean a bathroom. Don't expect perfection but it gets the point across at any age and scratches one more chore off your to do list.

*Do take-home work or read your industry magazines and trades while your children are doing their homework.

*As a family, walk the dog. It's amazing how much you learn about school during these walks which almost eliminate the dead silence after the dreaded "What did you do at school today?" interrogation.

*Run, bike, or walk around the field while the kids are at their soccer, baseball or football practice. (Wave now and then.)

*Do much of your grocery shopping at the farmers market and bring the kids. Let them pick out their own fruits and vegetables. Pick up some popcorn and let them chose your flowers.

*Turn off the T.V and read, as a family, in one bed, at night. No matter what age your kids are.

*Pack your own lunch or snacks while making the kids' lunch. A prepared and proportioned diet is easier to stick to than leaving it to your own discretion when it's noon and you're already starving, especially if you are at home. Load both lunches up with fruit and vegetables.

Make up your own harmonizing activities and try to involve the kids as much as possible. You don't need "quality time" if you just experience everyday activities together. You don't need numerous play dates if you engage your children in your life and come down to their level. Use your imagination and encourage your children to do the same. Not all games have to be a structured environment with rules. Not all chores have to be miserable or done by mom.

I

INTUIT: {To know or understand by a keen or quick insight. A direct perception independent of any reasoning process.}

Intuition is the God-given gift to women to make up for the injustice of existing in a male- ruled society and world. Actually, every person has intuition but women are more in sync with theirs.

The cyclical nature of the female biology is prone to a fine-tuning of the senses. Intuitive knowledge resides in the subtle senses and can only be heard by one who is sensitive towards these subtleties. Add the compassion a mother brings to the picture and I don't have to tell you how sharply those senses can be tuned.

Call it a gut feeling, an inner voice, a guardian angel, direct knowing, an instinct, a sixth sense, or down right clairvoyance, whatever- - -but your intuition connects the mind-heart push-me-pull-me that constantly plays out in the female drama. Your mother's intuition is often the first time you begin taking this second voice seriously, but it can be refined to all areas of your life.

Follow that intuition. Its your higher soul speaking the course of good and elevation. It's the song of the invisible thread of life weaving it's voice into your consciousness- -sometimes subtle, often overbearing. Don't listen to it and it either goes away or comes back with a forceful vengeance, capable of destroying hardened convictions or saving lives. Nurture it and it grows like a lovely garden of clear thought and deeper wisdom. Your intuition is the unconditional love that keeps knocking on the door of your inner dialogue. It's up to you to open the door and accept the kind conversationalist.

Intuit your life song and add background music to the score you are constantly composing. It adds rich dimension and balance to an information-overload perspective.

Note times when you did and didn't listen to your intuition. Even small examples like should I drive that way to work? Or, I knew that restaurant meal was bad but ate it anyway. What about when you worried about your child at the same time she later reported a tummy ache, in school, miles away from you? Register the outcomes. Was your intuition correct? Was it trying to steer you clear of small disasters or bad judgments? Did it tune you in to possible problems?

We are taught to be rational, think with facts and empirical knowledge and believe only what we see, but the world is neither black nor white and, in this age of super-sophisticated technology, we don't always see the things that help us so much. Like invisible cell phone connections, our intuition is there, waiting to be picked up by the satellite of our thoughts. Can you HEAR ME NOW?

J

JOY: {Intense and especially ecstatic or exultant happiness. The overflow of a thankful heart.}

Joy-That Christmas-time feeling! That gooey-good happiness thick with meaningful emotion, reserved for angels and saviors. Well, I say mothers are the angels and saviors of the earth-bound type and we should make it our responsibility to spread the joy down here, all year round.

You don't need a holiday, an earth changing message or a corny dedication to be a joy- mongering mom. You just need to share it when you get it and you usually get in the small details of motherhood: The first smile, the first steps, the journal entry, the sleeping child, the home run, the hugs and kisses, the good report card. Joyful, meaningful theatre is going on around you all the time. Photograph it, record it, replay it and package it up to give away and share.

With the fatigue and routine of motherhood, the celebration of firsts in our children's lives, are exclamation points in the day-to-day, which are sometimes overlooked. They often fade with time and age and we lose something important in the process--like our children's innocence. Our kids are thrown into such a false maturity that, when actual adulthood seeps in, they are totally unprepared.

Recapture the joy of childhood through our children's milestones. Let them linger in the air of the breath of our memories and carry them inside us, ready to call on at any moment. Be ready to exhale all their goodness, simplicity and purity into the universe we live in. Share these "first" joys with our elders and with the young ones we are mentoring, therefore elongating their existence. Play them back to our families to preserve them and to use them as building blocks for traditions and stories and good feelings about belonging and importance, self-esteem and life cycles. Joy to the world. Joy to the universal cycle of things. Joy to moms who constantly propel that cycle forward.

K

KINDNESS: {The act or state of being kind.}

Considered one of the seven virtues, there is great power in kindness. It is something we are all capable of and we are given numerous opportunities, daily, to exercise kindness. It's invaluable in raising children and competing in business. Its roots are based in family (kind) but it's branches reach out to society.

What we display in charity and kindness in action before our children's eyes is the singularly most important trait we can pass on to them.

Our society has put so much stress on competition, survival of the fittest and swimming with sharks that kindness has taken on an archaic image. We need to dust off that image and polish the golden qualities kindness entails. In our consumer-driven, me- oriented, myopic, get ahead, fast-paced race to win, we've sacrificed manners, politeness, charity and sympathy towards others and it has damaged us severely. Kindness crept out the door when electronic isolation barreled in, making it easy to avoid one-on-one contact and face-to-face interaction. Neglect kindness and we all suffer the harsh backlash.

Let's call for a kindness revolution, a get-ahead system based on kind acts, charitable causes and sympathy towards each other led by the mothers of the world whose innate understanding of selflessness can fuel it. Let's reward and promote employees based on a merit system geared toward kind behavior towards colleagues and clients alike as well as production levels and profit and loss. Imagine a conference room where kindness is seen as a sign of strength not weak female behavior. Let's do unto others in every aspect of our Cmom lives and watch our communities, families and workplaces, thrive. Kindness can unite in a very powerful way, and unity dissipates the need to do harm and injury to one another. By thinking, acting and speaking kindness we show our children a way to live based on the simplest of actions.

Kind actions and gestures can pull you out of the slump of non-importance, low self- esteem and depression. Next time your therapy session comes around, pass it up and take that $100 to buy 100 hamburgers for the hungry. Hand them out so you can experience the joy the kind act of feeding someone brings. Take your age-appropriate kids with you to *show* them charity and it will sink in much deeper than preaching at them. I guarantee this experience will leave you feeling better than any one-hour shrink session. You instantly feel better about yourself, your situation and your own life. It's experiential and hard to explain but I did this once a week in the downtown area where I worked for years. The return on investment was amazing. I brought interested friends, my child, my husband and my coworkers and I know firsthand that my immediate financial successes had a lot to do with feeding those less fortunate. Kindness karma is instantaneous so plant your kindness crop daily and watch your harvest multiply.

L

LOVELINESS: {A beauty that appeals to the heart and mind as well as to the eye. A quality that gives pleasure to the senses.}

Even the word loveliness itself is desirable, with its smooth O's, soft L's and divine V. Of course it embodies love and all moms embody love too.

But do you generate loveliness? Do you exude love from every pore and essence of your being? Do you personify loveliness in sight, sound, touch, taste and smell? Do moms spend time any more on being lovely?

Our femininity has gone through such a cultural redesign that loveliness has been all but replaced by an overt sexuality whose expiration date is extremely limited. This commercial-born, Hollywood-hyped, magazine-managed image of beauty is constricting and impossible to maintain. By working on our own personal loveliness we regenerate our inner beauty thereby reviving an endless fountain of youth that is so often and incorrectly searched for outside ourselves. Loveliness is soul beauty.

Lovely is often used to describe beautiful nature in literature and it's naturally beautiful that the moms of the world personify this quality as the regenerators of humankind. C moms work better if they surround themselves with loveliness, so put effort and time into the lovely things and environments that make you feel love. Spend time in nature and take your children with you. Natural influences on our psyche and our children's psyche have countless positive effects. Plant a garden, care for it and watch it grow.

Make sure you have a personal space that is your ideal lovely spot. Embellish your space with things you adore, that make you feel good and that are pleasing to all of *your* senses. Hopefully, this space can even be your office. No matter where I've worked, I have gone to great lengths to make my surroundings as lovely as possible. It's amazing how this can affect coworkers, production output and a general sense of satisfaction in the work place. In fact, at one job, I was even having a problem with people wanting to stay too long in my office.

Looking lovely and exuding an air of loveliness helps your entire attitude and how people react to you. It affects whom you attract in your life on all levels and shows the world a self-confidence that comes from within. Remember that loveliness is a beauty that appeals to the heart and mind, not to the eye alone. If you are working on loving qualities with a sincerity of heart and discipline of mind, your own individual loveliness shines through.

Think of important times in a woman's life when she is said to be lovely. It often starts with a prom or similar event, followed by being a bride and then is usually associated with pregnancy. You probably have a visual of each of these occasions and it's not just how you physically looked or the way you were dressed that made you feel lovely but it was what you were experiencing inside that gave you that extra glow. Let's maintain that "glow" in our daily C mom lives by calling on our inner beauties to shine outwardly for the world to see and experience. The most defining quality of loveliness is that it is eternal and lasting because it derives from the natural best we can be.

M

MEDITATION: {Continued or extended thought or contemplation. Spiritual introspection.}

Meditation calms the hurricane of emotional, physical and mental activity of everyday living that moms experience. It surrenders the structure of inner speak and stream-of-conscience chatter to an unrestricted playground of possibility and contemplation.

Meditation induces the connection to Divinity and in so doing leaves remnants of that same Divinity behind to help you. Those divine "helpers" can be experienced as tranquility, illumination, bliss, luminosity, self-possession, focus, serenity, inner knowing, stamina, clarity and self-mastery. Who couldn't use a little of that?

I first learned to meditate when I was restricted to bed rest in the final month of my pregnancy. I had been working at a job that was twenty-four seven as the marketing director for a huge upscale mall. Needless to say, sitting in bed all day was a huge adjustment. I bought a book about meditation and speaking to your child while in the womb and helping the birthing process by concentrating on helping the baby and not on your own pain. Yeah right. I was bored and trapped in bed so I spent hours visualizing and meditating. When it was time to deliver, I did so naturally in 30 minutes and with no painkillers or epidurals. This was not by choice. It just turned out that way. That experience showed me how powerful the mind is and that meditation really *worked*. It was completely experiential. I am thankful to my son for that experience because if he hadn't wanted to come out early, I would have never learned to meditate. It's amazing what our children teach us if we are still and open enough to listen. Little did I know that was just the tip of the iceberg when it came to learning about meditation.

My second experience was much more deep and profound and meditation saved my life. I was at an all-time low going through a divorce and was desperate enough to go see a clairvoyant. She was amazing, spot-on and introduced me to a meditation called Twin Hearts Meditation. Meditating every day to this CD not only de-stressed me to the point where I could realize I was working myself into the ground, it focused me when I was depressed and unable to concentrate. It balanced my emotions that were angry, sad and confused--all at the same time. It made me get in touch with the real me. The me which had for so long, been silenced to the point of near extinction and dulled by too many glasses of wine. I remember crying openly and in public the first time I did this meditation in a class the same psychic taught, which if you knew me at the time was not part of my vocabulary or personal makeup. I was a tough ad exec in the competitive fashion industry impervious to girlie emotion. I cried because I had no idea what had happened to the part of me that was happy and optimistic.

I got to see a glimmer of that part of me that I loved while meditating. It opened my inner eye to my personal divinity and I vowed then and there never to lose it again.

I still do this meditation three to five times per week and have for the last ten years. I can't recommend it enough, however since meditation is such a personal self-reflecting process, whatever resonates with you and whatever type is going to make you stick with it, is the type you should incorporate into your daily routine.

Having your children see you meditate to deal with stress is priceless and sure beats the quick fix alternatives. I know meditation works because of the times I skip it. I feel my age, easily stressed and high-strung. My memory is not as sharp and my intuition is softened. I even look younger and more youthful when I meditate so if that's not a motivator I don't know what is.

NOURISH: {To cherish, keep alive or strengthen. To supply with what is necessary for life}.

Nourish your body, your soul, your life, your passion and hobbies, your children, your husband, your love, your family, your friends, your awake time and sleep time with healthy, living energy.

Use the simplistic, basic qualities life on Mother Earth gives us like: good air, clean water and sunshine. Focus on making sure these elements are sustainable for your children's futures and their children's futures. Participate in nourishing the biggest mother we know and practice green living. Nourish the earth to guarantee receiving her life-sustaining gifts for your own generation and for generations to come.

As mothers we understand the most basic necessity in life is nourishment because we are designed and self-contained to nourish our babies before they even arrive. Our feedings strengthen their bodies so they can grow and evolve. Something happens however, when time gets constrained and schedules get hectic, and before we know it, that bag of chips becomes our lunch and our kids are put on the fast food track of convenience.

As the major meal providers for the family, the present condition of our eating habits, are downright shameful. A dietary time-out is past due.

Let's nourish our children, ourselves and our families again. Let's take back the family dinnertime to detox from the day, share with our loved ones and enliven and revitalize our bodies to a healthful, vibrant state. Incorporating foods that are products of the forces of nature- water, light and air- into your C mom grocery list enables you to carry on the most innate and basic duty of providing nourishment.

Nourishing your body with food is important but we often forget how important the simple act of breathing can be for the body. Being aware of your breath, controlling it and slowing it down to a deeper level at least once or twice a day works wonders on the brain, emotions and of course the respiratory system. By oxygenating the body with deep breaths, vital nutrients are circulated to areas that have increased energy demands. Hectic, busy, C mom schedules don't need to be interrupted to practice deep, slow breathing. It can be done anywhere, anytime and it's free. Think of the impact taking the time for a deep breath before a stressful situation has on the child watching. Experience the calming effect that breath has on your reactions.

To love is to provide, to provide is to preserve.[1]

Let your nourishing acts rain down on your family to ensure healthy growth and longevity.

---

[1] Gmcks:3838 The existence of God is self evident

O

OPEN: {To expand. To render accessible. Relatively free of obstruction or barriers.}

Open your mind to new experiences and ideas. Face your fears and stretch outside the norm, the pigeonhole or the monotony that motherhood often brings. Open your eyes to changes and redefinitions of yourself and your role.

View the world with the open mind your young children possess and watch how the mundane and regular become suddenly magical. Open your heart to include a wider reach and inclusivity. Step outside your comfort zone and meet new worlds of existence and ways of being.

Depend on sources like public libraries, the Internet and new technologies to help you expand your horizons past your current capacity level. Read when your children read, study when your teens hit the books, visit new places, different cultures and make foreign friends. Be open in all aspects of your C mom life and make your life richer and more dimensional.

Globalization is the norm and our world is as diverse as ever. Your adaptability to new and different is key to your and your children's ability to thrive. By being open you lend yourself to easy adjustments and flexible corrections when things are beyond your control, therefore putting you in a stronger position of power when the need comes.

The mysteries of the mind are vast and complex and often its most powerful workings are hidden. Keeping the mind open to new perspectives and ideas enables you to alter your life accordingly based on ever-changing life experiences. You never know what you might unlock and find right up there in your own brain!

Nothing changes ones life more than the experience of becoming a mother. That's when the opportunity to experiment with being open to new ideas and methods is in full swing. I was working full time when I gave birth to my son and even timed his delivery with a lull in my business cycle so I wouldn't miss much work. When my son arrived, that was it. I fell totally in love with this new person, and blinded by that love, I called up my company and told them there was no way I was coming back to work, that they would have to accept my resignation. I was open to a whole new way of life, a new regimen and an entirely different lifestyle to accommodate the needs of my new baby.

Surprisingly, my company was open too and put me on a consulting-based agreement that enabled them to call me on *my* schedule and ask for my opinions regarding issues I specialized in. I even got a paycheck. Open your mind, open your heart and watch your world open up accordingly.

P

PRANA: {Life force or vital energy that permeates the body}.

Prana is the sacred energy that animates us from conception to end. Prana is the basis for all life and because it is often invisible, it lends mystery to our humanness. If we delve into that mystery and try to begin to understand prana and how to use it to our advantage, it increases our personal magnetism.

The source of prana is one of the most controversial subjects pertaining to human existence and there are too many opinions to go into detail here. Most of those opinions have their basis in religion and a belief in God. However, it doesn't matter what your viewpoint is on the source of prana in order to strengthen and increase your own supply of it. As long as you realize that you have energy that exists both inside and outside of the body and that this energy is dynamic and divine, you know about prana. Think of a sponge submerged in water wherein the water exists inside and outside of the sponge and you have the basic ideas of how prana functions.

Our bodies have the natural ability to heal themselves and our prana is vital in the healing process. By making our prana stronger, we become stronger, less prone to disease of the body and we function on a more efficient level. Most people understand that prana is connected to a higher, divine source. By increasing this connection to the source (whatever the belief system) we can strengthen our prana. By keeping our prana cleaned up, it gets stronger.

Here are some simple ways to keep your prana healthy and super strong:

-Try to avoid super negative emotions and situations as these suck the prana out of us, creating illness or fatigue. Replenish your prana with positive emotions and actions.

-Maintaining a connection to God or your spiritual source, religion or practice strengthens your prana. Prayer, for example.

-Cutting off other people's prana that intermingles with ours through normal interaction, at the end of the day, by using your intention or even using your hands to "slice" through or cut the connections from your own body, gives you an immediate rush of your own prana (looks funny but feels great and like a ton of bricks has been removed).

Have you ever walked into a room and immediately been brought down by the energy in the room? That's the prana other people have that may not be so positive or uplifting. Negative thoughts and emotions really effect prana. Some people are walking around in a bubble or aura of dirty prana all the time. Be alert to these people and situations and try to steer clear. Living in a big city is like floating around in a giant soup of everyone else's prana.

Try to escape now and then to less populated places where you can experience more of your own prana without the influence of everybody else. Nature is a good prana strengthener. So is exercise.

Kids have their own prana and teaching them to cut off from their school day (again with the funny slicing motion in front of the body and intent) helps them regenerate and strengthen their own life force. Watch your children's sick days disappear and the length and severity of their common illnesses decrease.

Think of all the inventions and amazing things science has given us. There is one thing science cannot do: it cannot make a flower. No amount of life animation or technology can reproduce a flower. The same is true for us and every other living thing. It's prana that enlivens us-and the flowers, and by being aware of your prana you connect to its divine magic.

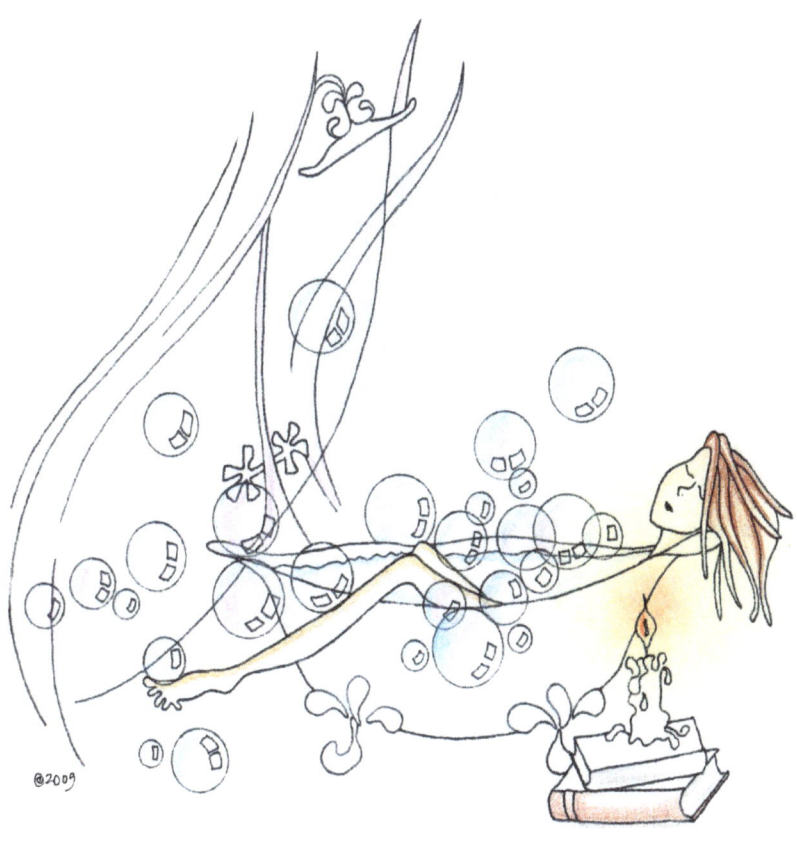

Q
QUIETUDE: {The state of being quiet; Tranquil}.

Quietude is scarce for busy, active C moms. The cacophony of family, work, friends, sports, recreation, driving here, going there, reading this and computing that, mending tears, kissing bumps, garbage trucks and talking news, the dog, the neighbors, the mailman and grocery stores, voicemail and passwords, the minivan and recess, coffee pots and dishwashers, office jokes and traffic jams, TVs and video games--it's time to turn the volume OFF!

Rest in quietude. Hear your own thoughts and listen to the peacefulness of silence. Distraction comes in many forms and the impact that noise has on our ability to focus is subtle and often undetected. We wonder why our kids have trouble in quiet classrooms and why we have a nationwide epidemic of attention disorders. Are we training our kids to depend on background noise?

Quieting down our lives and homes quiets our kids to help their attention spans grow and their concentration to focus. Schedule quiet time way beyond the preschool years. Use it as treasured family time. Set aside blocks of time where the entire family participates in quiet time. It could be a night, a week, or an hour a day. No electronics, no games, no computers, no ear buds or iPads, no isolation from each other, no phones, no distractions. Experience being-without all the bells and whistles. Practice quietude to muffle the blaring interruptions that divert our attention and fragment our focus. Use quietude to limit mental stress, which results from noise-based distractions.

The gift of gab is female in nature and the ability to communicate frequently and often is a treasure, but taking the time to be silent is beneficial too. Stilling speech quiets the thoughts and C moms can practice temporary vows of silence to achieve a clearer mind, controlling the incessant chatter of thought that calms when we close our mouths for short periods. You don't have to be a monk to benefit from being quiet or thinking before you speak!

The byproduct of incessant chatter is gossip. Its growth by way of the internet is staggering and the harm it does in our schools, sometimes even deadly. Limiting gossip time to use for personal quiet time not only benefits your own friendships and the way other people perceive you but it shows by example how control over your speech is helpful in avoiding damage to others. C moms teach their children that silence truly can be golden.

REVIVE: {To make active, to set in motion or restore to life. To renew to a flourishing condition}.

Revive what you love about yourself. Revivify self-approval. Revitalize the essence of your being that pleases you beyond words. Fill in the blank "I love myself when I am_____."

Awaken your happiness and personal pleasure. Cultivate your contentment whatever that may be. There is no better time than now to remember your rapture.

For me it's running. It sounds dumb but I love who I am when I am pounding down a certain hill to the beach on a run I have done for the last 18 years. I always have my favorite tunes on and I am oblivious to the outside world. There's something about the freedom, the ocean, the sunlight, and the physicality of running that all come together for me in pure bliss. The feeling afterward is complete contentment. Only the hill and I exist and I get ecstatic. It goes far beyond a runner's high. I get lost and the responsibilities of my life temporarily fade away. I escape, just for a while, but it's long enough to revive me into a happier version of myself. It empowers my life in an indescribable way and my butt benefits too.

I've run that hill before my wedding and pushed baby joggers up and down it after my pregnancy. I've missed it on business trips and craved it when I was injured. I've solved strategic work issues while running and broken through emotional hurdles and personal problems too. It's my passion and, like most personal passions moms have, it ends up on the bottom of the to do list, often ignored and put on hold for everybody else's needs.

Revive your passion. Push it up to the top of the list of things to do today. Make it a priority. Schedule it in. Make sure you even remember what it is that you love to do that is uniquely yours. It may be dancing, or doing your hair differently or playing that instrument you haven't picked up since you grew out of that band uniform. It could be as simple as sleeping in or singing in the shower. Whatever it is, revive it and activate it back into your life. You have to take the time to enjoy the things that are exclusive to you without the family, without the kids. The happiness you derive from your personal revivals will resonate with those close to you who love you and find pleasure in seeing you happy.

Look within to fulfill your pleasures and take the pressure off your husband, friends and children, all of whom you may be always looking towards to *make* you happy. Do your happy thing for self-acceptance, self-approval and contentment and those material things and must haves may not seem so shiny or even necessary. Watch all areas of your life flourish when you revitalize from your own source. Be satiated with self-restoration.

S

SPIRITUALITY: {Connection to a reality greater than oneself. Development of the inner life through certain practices.}

The presence of spirituality in a C mom's life eliminates the feelings mothers have, from time to time, of solitude or of being utterly alone.
Having a personal relationship with Divinity taps into the Source that sustains creation.

Maintaining the connection to the Divine through spiritual practices and rituals keeps the gap between mind, body and spirit close, balanced and edited. Your private relationship with the All-knowing is an important coping strategy that can pull you out of emptiness, fear of the future and the deep down lows.

Omnipresent love humbles us and in this humility we transcend the limitations of the material world. Hope becomes attainable. The impossible becomes possible and through faith in a loving power greater than our own we can achieve amazing things in life. The psychological barriers of the limits of our mortality are lifted if we just choose to link up to the power of Divinity. Like motherly love, Divine love is unconditional, unwavering and infinite.

Nurture your spirituality while cultivating its meaning and importance within your family. As the keeper of the family rituals, holidays and religious celebrations, make it your role to infuse your special events with spiritual sumptuousness. Use symbolic gestures and icons to explain history, meaning and traditions. Get creative and decorate your home with familiar spiritual motifs or themes to help your children understand the stories behind the symbols, seasons and celebrations and to remind you of the glory of Supreme goodness and beauty. Try to stay true to the real meaning of ceremony and minimize the commercial tone the holidays have.

Do research to explain to your children what the symbolism behind your practices means and let them help make new family traditions based upon what they learn, what resonates with them or interests them. Spiritual rituals done from and with the heart are meaningful and have a long lasting impression on good judgment and right actions.

Spend time pursuing your spirituality. Talk to your source often and confide frequently. It's great to have somewhere to entrust your deepest desires, wishes and private matters. Participate in your spiritual community to share with like-minded members.

Respect and acknowledgment for Divinity brings meaning, order and a higher purpose to our C mom lives

T

TRANSFORMATION: {Change in form, appearance, nature or character.}

The transformation into motherhood is a radical one, and it's the best example of human adaptation and boundless possibility. Let it remind you of how enterprising and daring your life can be.

Don't take surviving motherhood for granted. Herald its triumphs, challenges and everyday victories and apply the same courage and guts to new, life-altering paths that come your way. Take the brave caterpillar approach and watch the butterfly emerge.

Transformation is exciting and challenging and stimulates you for adventure and growth.

I was comfortable running a small, downtown, single-loft branch of a worldwide publishing company that was based in Germany. The boss was oceans away, my editors were angels and I picked whom I wanted to work with. I came to the office in jeans everyday and logged in my own hours. I manifested this business lifestyle and it paid and functioned pretty darn well. Six years of doing it my way and in a thriving business climate. Then I got headhunted, to the biggest publishing corporation in the U.S. for a key executive position, with two titles!

Talk about transformation. From the hair that needed a new style to the business wardrobe, to holding my own against the boys club of MBA's, (which I don't have) and Harvard grads, a few multimillion dollar portfolios of clients, an entire editorial department that hated my sheer existence and a staff that promptly moved out of my department when I was hired. Oh, also the entire city of Los Angeles watching daily and the media business historically tanking.

A major transformation to say the least, but how invigorating.

On the job, I surrounded myself with guess what? :a group of other moms.
I knew moms were the most creative, transformational agents of change I could put into position to help me. We had a big thing in common and that similarity created strong loyalties and unchallengeable enthusiasm for our goals. We created one of the most successful small teams the business had seen in years and not only did this huge change transform my personal life, it also transformed a major way the 130 year old company I worked for did business.

I also transformed the way I dealt with the boys-only club and proposed to my future boss that I take Fridays off early to go to my son's football games. It was his first time playing football and I wanted to make sure it was a good experience for him. I had no idea about football and still really don't. The point is, I appealed to the male side of my colleagues as opposed to asking for "mom" time. My boss told me if I didn't go home early on Fridays, I couldn't have the job! He loved repeating the story at business dinners when bragging about my negotiation skills. Transformation! Right down to the testosterone level.

I was the first female publisher ever at the company and enjoyed many firsts for myself, my team, my clients and for a whole new department of editors and business launches. It was challenging, daring, exhausting and exhilarating all at once and if I wasn't up to the task with the ability to be extremely flexible and chameleon-like, I would have crashed and burned quickly.

The entire experience mirrored new motherhood in a strange and familiar way because of the transformation process. Inspiration, bravado, love, dedication, trial and error, and a sense of fulfillment were the fundamental similarities.

So go for it. Transform the situations that keep you in a rut. Transform the relationships that hold you back or no longer serve your goals. Transform your outlook on where you stand in the world and what your purpose is. Transform out of bad habits and old patterns. Transform your character to reflect who you truly want to be. Transform yourself into the parent that creates healthy well-rounded children. Transform your body into the expression of beauty you want to portray to the world, not the other way around. Step up to the challenge of transformation. Change is the only constant so you may as well master the art of transformation sooner than later.

U

UNITY: {The state of being one; oneness.}

We are all one and united in this thing we call life so we may as well act like it. Unity is the bond that strengthens our communities and families and we can accomplish great things when we are in unison with each other.

We teach our children to treat others like they want to be treated because we understand the basic foundation of our interconnectedness, but let's make sure we appreciate the spirit of unity and the strength it has in our lives.

No matter how independent you are, you can't do it totally alone. Everyone needs help now and then, a motivational partner, someone to bounce ideas off of, pick up the slack, compliment your qualities, accommodate for your shortcomings and share the pain along with the pleasure. Unity builds closeness, loyalty and an appreciation for coming together to accomplish the task at hand. We're talking Big Picture thinking here where separateness is an illusion we can't afford to keep buying into. How much more motivated are you when your morning walking club is waiting for you even though you don't want to put on your shoes? What kind of money do you raise when you get a group of like-minded parents involved to pay for that new playground? Who benefits when you volunteer to sit on the city council to make your town more productive?

Unity doesn't deny individuality. It respects every individual and the uniqueness that each one brings to the table. So get together and unite with fellow moms. Take the initiative and not only lead that group but create one. Look for opportunities to connect and cooperate with others to reach common goals and take advantage of the skills and talents in the people around you that can enhance your project outcome. If the proverbial boulder is blocking your path to success, maybe it's time to incorporate unity into your plan and take advantage of fine tuning your work with outside input and group effort. Bounce your ideas off a casual gathering of friends and meet often to be a sounding board for them. You don't have to be a Mensa member to start your own mini think tank and enjoy the social and intellectual interaction your group can provide. You don't have to be managing a workforce to be a team player.

Our mothers knew the value of bridge and book clubs, bowling leagues and bake sales, sewing circles and potlucks. They pooled their forces around a common interest and not only expanded their horizons but built lifelong friendships and experiences that lasted well into the twilight years. So don't go it alone. Get involved, join now, sign up, volunteer and contribute to the whole. Your skills and talents are needed and in a bigger context than you can accomplish by yourself. None of us is as good as all of us and you could be the missing puzzle piece that puts it all together for a group that needs your unique gifts. C moms unite and claim your greatness.

V

VIGILANCE: {The quality of being watchful or alert. Devotionally attentive and awake.}

Vigilance is the discipline necessary to see things through and it's the first and final phase of developing your ideal life scenarios. Vigilance gives you the focus to succeed so you don't run out of steam when you arrive towards the end of your goals.

It should motivate you with the same enthusiasm you had when you began your important undertakings as when you accomplish or finish them. Vigilance takes dedication; patience and an attention to detail that is laser sharp. It's not easy because it takes willpower and good old-fashioned hard work.

Attend to your life with a vigilance worthy of a good hand maiden. Pay attention to the details of the day-to-day because those are the things that make the sum total of a life well lived. Moms are so consumed with the well being of their children's lives that they frequently neglect their own needs. Constant vigilance keeps you on track and focused. Moms are especially equipped to withstand the toughest of vigils. Newborn sleep cycles are a true testimony to motherhood vigilance; so is potty training, tending to childhood illnesses, role modeling good behavior and manners, late night vigils for driving age teens, and college entrance submissions.

No matter what type of circumstances C moms currently live under, special vigilance should be given to the following:

*The health and general well being of the only body you have to live this life in. No excuses. Women neglect their own health at a catastrophic rate once they finish with the childbearing process. Get physicals, visit your gyno and participate in age-appropriate health tests and screenings.

*Finances. If you have a spouse that takes care of all financial matters, help him out and be informed about what your family financial picture truly is. You never know when you need to be the one to handle the money and you might as well get up to speed now. If you are actively involved in managing your own finances stay on top of current markets, rates and investment options to maximize your assets. Control useless debt and minimize your exposure in case of emergencies. Know your tax status and filings and the details of your latest tax return.

*Insurance policies. Health, life, financial, auto and home insurance are necessary evils of modern living. Read your policies so there are no surprises when you least expect them. Shop for new policies and competitive pricing models for your ever-evolving parental status. Make sure you have updated information from your job on guidelines and benefits to take advantage of pricing and discounts. Get informed on how you are and are not covered.

*Your Resume. Even if you're not looking for a job, or aren't working, have a current resume on hand always, so you can be prepared for that next big opportunity. Update your profile to include new skills and talents. Have a good and current headshot picture on hand preferably in a pdf format so you can transmit your image over the Internet at a moment's notice. With all the technology available it's easy to create your own "about me" file that best describes your talents and skills whether you are currently working or haven't held a job since college. Surprise yourself by listing your special qualities and be prepared to sell yourself in writing if the need or opportunity comes up.

Being vigilant with these basic (and I'll admit boring and tedious) details can eliminate big problems in the future that you may not see coming. Vigilance here gives you knowledge and power when faced with emergency situations, better preparing you for fast, quick-on-your feet decision making in times of tragedy or disaster or for opportunity and once-in-a-lifetime chances.

Vigilance is difficult and takes fortitude and discipline, so when you're about to give up or throw in the towel, just remember the penguin incubation period in the harshest of Arctic climates and know that these funny tuxedoed parents haven't even figured out that their wings are for flying!

WISDOM: {Knowledge, intuitive understanding or insight. Discernment or experience.}

Wisdom is the culmination of all the qualities in the C mom work encyclopedia, applied. It's direct knowing and it comes from the heart and the mind. It's not just book study or IQ.

Wisdom is applied experience through learning the lessons of your mistakes the first time around. It's the ability to recognize the good and the just because those are the qualities that you cultivate within yourself.
Wisdom is the reward for living in the realm of the moral and ethical. When you generate goodness in your life, your ability to see the world clearly is sharpened and missteps and poor judgments become fewer and fewer.

Your head is at the very top of your body because that's the part of your body that *should* be in control. It's on top of your body and it's the closest to heaven. Your sex, guts and even your heart, are all housed below your head for a reason. Your brain is there to convert your lower energies into higher experiential knowledge or wisdom. It's there to regulate emotions and feelings as well as passions, habits, desires, wants and moods. If you let these lower energies run your life, you have total chaos. If you rely first and foremost on your brain and the wisdom it has accumulated to manage your life, you are light years ahead of people entrapped by their lower natures.

Increase your personal wisdom by practicing wholesome and upright behaviors. Intelligence is dependent upon a well-rounded and accurate view of things. If you misguide other people you too will be misguided. If you obstruct the truth from others the truth will be obstructed from your view. On the other hand if you use a moral compass to guide you, you'll be led in the right direction. Proper decision-making will be easier, good choices will be clearer to see.

Give yourself time to accumulate your wisdom. Backtrack to correct your mistakes but move forward afterwards. Bad judgments and miscalculations are there to help wisdom mature as long as the lessons are learned the first time around. If they aren't they usually appear in much more intense forms until we finally "get it". Spend time on trying to figure out why common mistakes keep happening and take the corrective actions to remedy the situation. The last thing you want to do is ignore your mistakes and miscalculations. Ignorance is the exact opposite of wisdom so be mindful of what you choose to *not* know. By taking responsibility for your mistakes and trying to find a solution in correcting them, the experience gained is stash away in your wisdom vault for the next time you are challenged with the same situations. Usually, when you think you have a certain negative trait mastered, it comes after you again with a vengeance, so it's nice to have a big cache of wisdom stock to pull out when you need it. After a while, the similar challenges will stop coming up because it's been ingrained in your brain on how to deal properly.

Wise men (or in this case women) aren't born. They are trained by the forces of nature and are necessary to overcome certain negative traits inherent in the individual. Don't resist the forces, face them head on and defeat them. Become wiser with time and experience the fruits of your lesson-learned labors. Isn't it wonderful that the capacity to keep learning is not limited to age? Be thankful that you are given the opportunity to overcome certain negative tendencies so that you can ascend to the wistful heights of sageness.

X

EXPLORE: {To look into closely, investigate or examine something new.}

Explore all your options. Let go of limitation. Travel beyond the boundaries. Penetrate the possibilities and live on the road less travelled if that's what your true calling harkens.

C moms face multiple decisions daily and deep exploration into unfamiliar options can lead you to amazing discovery and unchartered territory chock full of potentiality.

Exploration takes a certain amount of courage, so put your brave boots on and begin your march towards adventure. Dive in and explore every aspect of your current life as a mother, a woman and a world citizen.

Visit areas of neglect to see where you can improve your life. Begin with the simple and advance to the more complex. For example, explore your daily schedule and then move up to your weekly, then monthly schedule, routine and activities. Notice open gaps of time available for adjustments. Fill those gaps with meaningful activities that expand your horizons and make a difference in your life, your family life and your community. Explore within yourself to find out what really matters to you and put your energies into developing those personal causes.

Turn off the autopilot and really get involved. Moms get so bogged down with parental tasks they risk a life full of *going through the motions* and not really experiencing living to the fullest extent. Before you know it, your kids are grown and you have no idea what happened to the last twenty plus years.

Self-exploration is an exhilarating way to keep inventing your ideal mom life. Be honest with your self-exploration and get to know your weaknesses and your strengths. Give yourself a birds-eye view of how you are really living your life so you can have objective and realistic insight. You may find that your motivations and goals have changed so keep altering and exploring new perspectives to freshen up your aims. Make a point of checking in with your current ambitions to be sure they fit in with the dynamic course of life that constantly alters. Have your children outgrown a stage that you seem to still be nurturing? Is your job static and unfulfilling because you've matured out of it? Do you still have the same hairdo you had from high school and are you still plucking those eyebrows in the same way? Is your home baby-proofed even though your youngest child is entering high school? Does your garage look like a Toys R Us yard sale when your kids are all playing team sports? When was the last time you went new lingerie shopping for yourself, let alone your husband? Look around and peek into all areas of your life with your eyes wide open. Discover where you are in every stage and in every facet of your C mom life.

I was a newly divorced mom with a very stringent idea of how the next 15 years of my life were going to be managed. Nothing would come before the priority of my child. Every action stemmed from this idea and every decision, thought and moment in my life was dictated by placing my child first and foremost. I put him at the center of my universe and he was god, dictator and the essence of every breath I took. Sounds insane even as I write it but I was intent on not letting my mistakes mess up his upbringing and I thought at the time that this was the best strategy and that lightening up on any part of it was selfish and irresponsible. Then one of life's curve balls got thrown my way. I received a phone call after a meeting I attended from an acquaintance who proceeded to inform me that a certain gentlemen she knew, who was also there, was interested in meeting me. No way. Not in my vocabulary. I never put a relationship into my 15-year equation. Not in the plan at all. Sorry. But she was persistent, continuously vouching for him, singing his praises and assets and endlessly trying to persuade me to let him call me himself.

Her prodding was becoming annoying so I spent some time mentally deliberating and exploring all the reasons why I should withhold my phone number and remain aloof. It occurred to me that during this time he remained respectful of my decision not to engage. He could have found out on his own how to track me down but he didn't cross that line. I gathered my courage and acquiesced because I rationalized to myself that a phone conversation wouldn't be the end of the world and I could cut it off at any time. We spoke and something about his voice felt familiar and right and we scheduled a lunch to meet face to face. No time taken away from my son, just missing a boring salad bar with co-workers.

That lunch was the beginning of a long and wonderful journey that is still in process. He posed a simple question to me that changed my entire plan of self-inflicted martyrdom. "Don't you deserve to be happy?" I explored this simple idea for the first time in my life and spent a lot of time delving into the depths of its meaning to me and to my child. Didn't my son deserve a happy mom? Needless to say, years of "closet" dating and mom demands as well as tremendously long commutes put this new man through the paces worthy of military standards. I fell deeply in love with his commitment and effort as well as insanely in love with him. After six years he proposed when my son and I were ready and we are a happily married family. He is an eager stepfather and the love and bond between my two guys is amazing. I can finally say I am truly happy. Explore all your options and be courageous enough to live the best life you can have.

Y

YOUTHFULNESS: {Characterized by the condition of being young, the appearance of freshness and vigor.}

Youthfulness is the state of mind that says no matter where you are in your life; today is the day you are going to begin anew. Youthfulness gives you the optimism to look forward to your next big thing while invigorating your attitude with can-do energy.

Your mom world is in constant motion and it is here that things are really active and alive. It's the perfect place and time to tap into that liveliness and become part of the perpetual action that connects you to really feeling alive and well. Youthfulness here means it's never too late.

It's never too late to get that job or become a stay at home mom. It's never too late to go back to school or learn that secret skill you've always yearned to develop. It's not too late to volunteer or run for office. It's never too late to say, "I'm sorry" or "I love you".

It's not too late to run that marathon or climb that mountain. You still have time to write that book, paint that portrait, plant that garden, build that dream house, take the kids to Europe, get certified, learn the computer, save for a rainy day, start that diet, run your own business or go to that dancing class.

Time is on your side if you just get the ball in motion to move towards your dreams and goals. Take the first step today and stop putting off the things you've wanted to manifest for so long now. When you were younger your point of view was less cynical and your pessimism was underdeveloped. It was easier to go for it and see where life took you. You risked more and chance was a friend. So rediscover your youthful daringness and begin to fulfill your destiny.

Engaging now and taking action towards your dream stimulates your whole system and your step gets lighter, your attitude gets more appealing and magnetic to others and your happiness returns. There's nothing like a simple happy face to give you a younger appearance. There's nothing more youthful than a proper sense of self that exudes from every pore. There are so many products out on the market aimed at delivering our youth back to us on a silver platter. None of them take into account the fact that your demeanor and attitude have everything to do with it. None of the beauty products I've tried ever guaranteed my inside happiness or my youthful ambitions. You can't nip or tuck or plump or cream your way to the fountain of youth forever but you can be young at heart by acting out your dreams every day of your life.

Sacrificing everything, as a mother, is short sighted because eventually you run out of energy. Save a little for yourself and elongate the years you have for motherhood. Don't forget you get to do it all over again with your grandchildren and you want to be as young and as full of vivacious energy as possible when that time comes. Happier moms are healthier moms and healthier moms stay around longer to see the fruits of their labor (and labors) ripen into whole new families. Your constantly fresh approaches to life keep you always ahead of the mom game and you become a better asset to your children and family. A burnt-out and exhausted individual that never took time to learn something new or engage for herself is often surprised when life goes south as soon as the children are gone. Don't be stranded on that lonely island. Exercise your right to pursue your passions at any age and utilize your youthfulness for years to come.

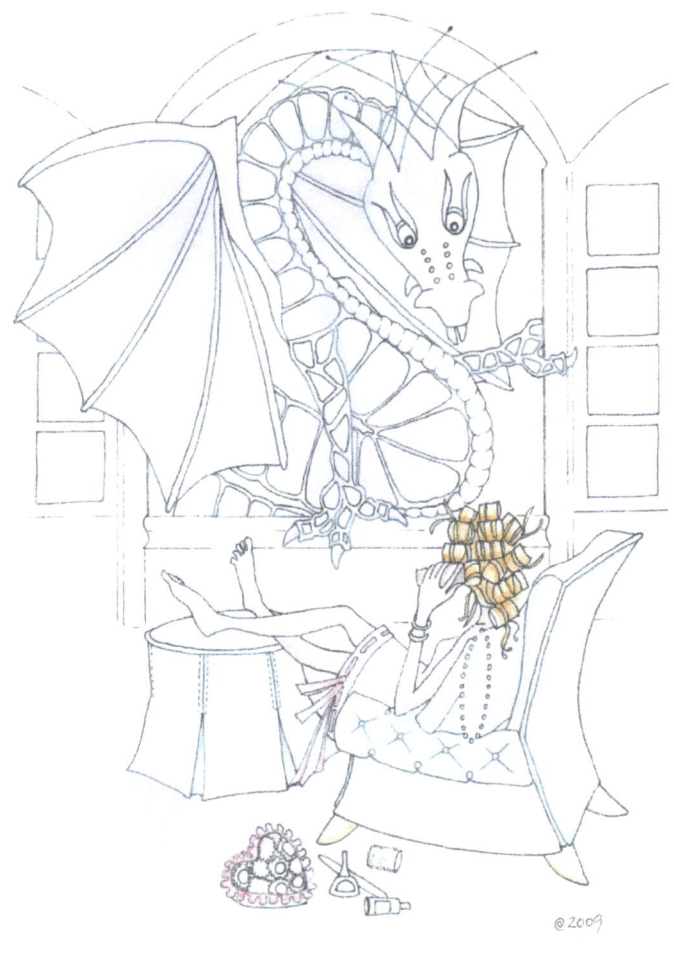

Z

ZERO: {Having no measurable quality. No, none, nil, zilch, zip.}

Zero fear. Zero guilt. Zero hate. Zero procrastination. Zero falsity. Zero revenge. Zero laziness. Zero evil and maliciousness. Zero degradation. Zero dishonesty. Zero self-loathing. Zero regret. Zero, zilch, zip, nil, none, nada.

None of these traits are in the C mom vocabulary, as they have no measurable quality in pursuing the ideal C mom life. They contribute nothing of value and hinder progress. They are to be avoided at all costs, red flagged and sent to your eternal trash bin of things you no longer need. Edit them out of your consciousness and overcome them by being busy with your aspirations. Delete them and replace them with your dreams. Give them zero time and attention. It's as easy as ABC.

Zero excuses not to live your ideal C mom life right now, to the full potential your Soul was meant to achieve.

To be continued...

C mom work®2009   www.Cmomwork.com

www.ingramcontent.com/pod-product-compliance
Lightning Source LLC
LaVergne TN
LVHW010018070426
835512LV00001B/5